M000043983

Find True North

written and illustrated by
Douglas Wood

 A Wind In The Pines book

Adventure Publications, Inc.
Cambridge, Minnesota

Dedicated...

To all who love the North and the feel of a
paddle in their hands.

Illustrations by Douglas Wood
Book design by Jonathan Norberg

Copyright 2005 by Douglas Wood

Published by Adventure Publications, Inc.
820 Cleveland St. S
Cambridge, MN 55008
1-800-678-7006
Printed in China

ISBN-13: 978-1-59193-131-7
ISBN-10: 1-59193-131-2

To the Reader:

A canoe trip is life distilled, and the canoe itself a near perfect vehicle for encountering the landscape. A canoe trip will provide sunsets, moonrises, storms, easy stretches, hard portages, big waves, fast water, flat water, wildlife, fear, joy, beauty, misery, and a thousand other things - each to be encountered and experienced, not observed or avoided. Just like the Big Trip.

As a medium of travel and education, the canoe has four great advantages. It is quiet, it's simple, it's beautiful, and you have to move it yourself.

The fact that a canoe is quiet encourages quiet within the paddler, and means you can sneak up on shy things. Its simplicity imparts great clarity to the lessons you learn while in a canoe. Its beauty makes you *want* to be in it, and adds grace to your journey. The fact that you move it yourself means that you must provide the intent, the skill, and the elemental power for any direction or progress to be achieved, and this is good for the paddler in countless ways.

From one who loves canoes and everything about them to those who feel the same...good paddling.

—*Douglas Wood*

3

Simplicity.
Silence.
Beauty.

Join in.

Think while you paddle.

Don't think while you paddle.

Sneak up on things.

9

10

KISS
(Keep it simple, stupid.)

Remember...there's more to life than increasing its speed.

Keep a weather eye.

Pick a spot on the horizon
and hold to it.

Some simple rules:

Either paddle or drift.
Lean too far, you tip over.
Scout a rapids before
      you run it.
Quiet if you want to see
      shy things.

Pick blueberries.
Pick pretty campsites.

Leave a place better than
you found it.

Remember...no matter how
cold and wet you are,
you're always warm and dry.

Tend your campfire.

Pack more under your hat
than in your pack.

Learn to read sign.

Make friends with solitude.

Keep your tent lines tight.

Look up.

Keep your matches dry.

Scrub your pots.

When you're tired, sleep.
When you're hungry, eat.

Play with otters.
Don't bother bears.

Smile on portages.

Feel the earth turn.

Listen.

Let beauty seep in.

Collect moonrises.

Run fast water when you can.
Portage when you should.

Be a part of things.

Know that you *are* a part of things.

When you see clearly,
things are just as they are.
When you do not see clearly,
things are just as they are.

Try to see clearly.

47

Learn lessons from
rocks and stumps and...
everything.

Know that a map is not
the territory.

Explore the territory.